HOW TO RAISE AND TRAIN A
GREAT DANE

By LINA BASQUETTE

Distributed in the U.S.A. by T.F.H. Publications, Inc., 211 West Sylvania Avenue, P.O. Box 27, Neptune City, N.J. 07753; in England by T.F.H. (Gt. Britain) Ltd., 13 Nutley Lane, Reigate, Surrey; in Canada to the book store and library trade by Clarke, Irwin & Company, Clarwin House, 791 St. Clair Avenue West, Toronto 10, Ontario; in Canada to the pet trade by Rolf C. Hagen Ltd., 3225 Sartelon Street, Montreal 382, Quebec; in Southeast Asia by Y.W. Ong, 9 Lorong 36 Geylang, Singapore 14; in Australia and the south Pacific by Pet Imports Pty. Ltd., P.O. Box 149, Brookvale 2100, N.S.W., Australia. Published by T.F.H. Publications, Inc. Ltd., The British Crown Colony of Hong Kong.

The photographer, Louise Brown Van der Meid, gratefully acknowledges the assistance of the following people for their help as models and with their dogs: Mr. and Mrs. Harold Henry, Mrs. Grace Smith, Mrs. James Daugherty, Mr. Roger Hopkins, Mr. and Mrs. Harold Hauser, Mr. Earl Braden, Handler Red Phillips, Miss Laura O'Day, Mr. and Mrs. Keith Kelsey, Mr. and Mrs. Sam Upton, Mr. John Martin, Mr. Downs and Mr. and Mrs. Gowin. The young models were Susan and Janet O'Brien, Mark and Kathy Daugherty and Lynne and Rob Van der Meid.

ISBN 0-87666-308-0

Copyright © 1961 by

TFH PUBLICATIONS, INC. P.O.Box 27, Neptune City, N.J. 07753
Manufactured in the United States of America
Library of Congress Catalog Card No.: 60-14332

Contents

Marge Champion, famous dancer and sister of the author, has found a new partner—a Great Dane from Miss Basquette's Honey Hollow Kennels in Chalfont, Pennsylvania.

1. History of the Breed

Ask any Great Dane owner why people who have Great Danes are usually nice, and he will probably give this stock answer: "Because we try to live up to our dogs."

The Apollo of dogs, this truly aristocratic, stately and graceful animal combines dignity and elegance with his great size and tremendous power. The Great Dane is a man's dog, a loyal friend rather than a pet. Yet he is also a woman's dog, with a strong protective instinct and a gentle and affectionate disposition.

The Great Dane seems to be well aware of his size, for as he pussyfoots around the house he never bumps into things, rarely considers himself a lap dog and hardly ever yields to the temptation to jump up on people. The only time he puts his great bulk to use against his friends is when a child gets too rambunctious and pulls his ears or jumps on his back. Then the Great Dane merely gets up, walks by the culprit and taps him lightly with his hip. But even before the stunned offender can pick himself up and squall, the Great Dane's immense tongue slops across the child's face, apologizing and forgiving, in the best parental manner.

A few years ago four children set out from their East Orange, New Jersey, home to see the world. The youngsters, accompanied by their Great Dane, got as far as Philadelphia before they were picked up and sent back home. When asked why they took the Great Dane with them, the eldest child answered, "We just couldn't be separated from our Dane forever, could we?"

Great Dane lovers claim that the dog possesses all the good qualities of the large breeds, plus all the smaller dogs' fine points, the only exception being that Great Danes can never be described as cute and cuddly.

THE GREAT DANE'S BACKGROUND

Just as people who are descendants of the original Mayflower passengers never tire of tracing their ancestry, so owners of Great Danes take pride in repeating the legends and telling the history of their animals. One of our oldest breeds, Great Danes have nothing to do with the country of Denmark. Instead, Germany takes credit for developing this particular breed.

As it is with so many of the older breeds of dogs, tracing the early history of the Great Dane is largely a matter of relying on legend, conjecture and guesswork, but most experts in the field of dog history believe that the Great Dane is a descendant of the huge Molossus seen on Greek and Roman statuary sculptured thousands of years ago. This is the original Mastiff, one of the world's basic breeds, probably most closely resembling the modern Tibetan Mastiff. Other authorities credit the Irish Wolfhound and Deerhound as the principal ancestors of the Great Dane. Best guess is that all these breeds (or their fore-bears) were involved.

At any rate, the Great Dane is ancient. In fact, there is a Greek coin minted in the fifth century which pictures a Dane-like dog. Dogs looking like Great Danes are also to be found on Egyptian monuments erected nearly 5000 years ago. Even the Chinese seem to have had Great Danes, or something very much like them, for a good description of a Great Dane can be found in a Chinese document dated 1121 B.C.

Somehow, probably through trading ships, Mastiff-like dogs found their way to England. And from there, according to ancient records, Romans exported hundreds of them for use in the circus ring to fight wild animals.

Officers in British provinces selected and trained these dogs to be sent to Rome, where for the amusement of spectators they were pitted against such animals as bears and lions. When these animals became scarce, bulls were substituted. Fortunately, the breed was never particularly bred for fighting bulls (bullbaiting, as it was later called), or our modern Great Dane might have a pushed-in, Bulldog face, with underslung jaw for holding tightly to bovine jowls.

It took the Germans, though, to develop the Great Dane as we know him today. In the 10th century, old German tribes put together a common forest and hunting law guide, collected under the title "Geoponica." In this, seven dogs were described, among them the Boarhound, the Bearcatcher and the Hare-hound. These offshoots of the Molossus (say most historians) were bred to British hunting dogs (probably forerunners of the Irish Wolfhound and Deer-hound), finally emerging as the present Great Dane some time around the 15th century.

These dogs, probably gray or steel-blue, were used mainly for hunting the wild boar, a ferocious animal that was then quite common in the duchies that are now part of Germany and Austria. The best Great Danes were said to have come from Stuttgart and Ulm.

During the next few centuries, while the breed was being refined and fixed, a number of noted personalities owned Great Danes—among them were Alexander Pope, the famous poet and translator; Charles V, emperor of Ger-many and King of Spain; Bismarck, German statesman and founder of the German empire (he had four Great Danes); and the Duchess of York.

The first pedigree that can be traced is to a dog named Nero I, born in Stutt-gart in 1876 and bred to Dr. Caster's Bella. There is also some record of a dog born in 1830, Luckey's Old Bob-tailed Countess, from which a line is said to have developed, though it seems to have been lost.

The first specialist club was formed in England in 1882 or 1883, and in 1888 a German club was formed.

In the meantime, Great Danes were being imported to America and, in 1877, thirteen dogs (called Siberian or Ulm dogs) were entered in a show in Philadelphia. The first U.S. Champion came ten years later. A Great Dane named Juno, import from Berlin, won the show for the Osceola Kennels, Osceola, Wisconsin.

In 1889, a group of 33 fanciers and breeders formed the American Specialty Club for Great Danes (known today as the Great Dane Club of America, with headquarters in New York). Two years later, the organization was admitted to the American Kennel Club, the fourth breed club to be admitted.

THE BREED'S NAMES

Why is the dog called a "Great Dane" when he has nothing to do with Denmark? We don't know for sure, but best guess is that the name comes from the old French designation *grand Danois*, which means "big Danish." Some early English writers say that the first dogs to be imported to England came from Denmark; a 1686 engraving by Richard Blome shows 13 Dane-like dogs hunting boar in Denmark. So, in some way, the dog was given its present name.

In non-English-speaking countries, however, the story is different. In addition to the French designation *grand Danois*, the dog was called *dogue allemand*, or "German Mastiff," the Mastiff designation encompassing a large group of big dogs particularly suited for hunting and fighting. When first given the name, the animal was one of only a dozen or so dogs distinctive enough to warrant a breed designation.

In Germany the breed was called all sorts of things. "Boar Hound" was used extensively in early times, as were the names "Fanghound," *Hatzrude, Saufanger* (literally, pig killer), *Altdeutsche Dogge* (old German Mastiff) and *Metzerghund* (butcher dog). More frequently they were given designations according to their color: *Ulmer Doggen* (from the city of Ulm) were brindles, *Danische Doggen* (Danish) were fawns and *Tiger Doggen* (named after the tiger-colored horse) were the harlequins.

In 1880 the Germans decided to do something about the confusion, and, under a famous judge named Dr. Bodinus, a meeting was called in Berlin at which it was decided that all names except *Deutsche Dogge* (German Mastiff) should be dropped forever. At the same time the breed was designated the national dog of Germany.

PERSONALITY

The Great Dane certainly deserves the title "The Continental Gentleman," for in spite of his awe-inspiring size, gentleness is probably his most noteworthy trait.

With children this is especially true. All of them have the tendency to experiment with their pets—to pull tails, poke, try to ride—and it's often cruel to let toddlers play with soft, tiny animals. But give a child a Great Dane to pal around with, and he'll develop a healthy respect. The dog often weighs as much as a robust human, so he can take punishment intolerable to a lesser animal. And if the child gets bothersome, the Great Dane simply walks away, aloofly ignoring the provoker, until begged to forgive. Only if extremely provoked will the Dane resort to retaliation, and even then he'll be careful not to inflict any real harm on his friend.

A marvelous guard dog with astounding good sense, the deeply inbred protective instinct serves to make the Great Dane a perfect guardian. One thing about a Great Dane—he doesn't have to show his muscle, just himself, to command respect.

Both young and adult Great Danes are wonderful pets for children—affectionate, reliable and able to take the poking and pulling that smaller dogs resent.

Nearly any dog makes a good watchdog, barking at trespassers and warning the family. But it takes a big and powerful dog to frighten a would-be felon, and a highly intelligent one to know enough not to jump lawful intruders, as thousands of long-suffering mailmen can attest.

In combat, the Great Dane is rarely, if ever, beaten. Although he will seldom attack a smaller dog, it is safer not to tempt him.

Regal gentleman that he is, a Great Dane will readily learn useful duties, but rarely condescends to learn parlor tricks. If you insist, he'll just stare at you with a look of disgust on his face.

Adaptable to apartment living as well as to farm life, the Great Dane is a true home dog, demanding to be part of the family, refusing to roam the streets unless there's no alternative. He is usually considered an excellent "fireside companion" and, more often that not, is purchased for the sole enjoyment and protection of the family. It's been a long, long time since he hunted the wild boar.

Most prospective Great Dane owners want a dog for a pet. They are prepared to make him a member of the family and will lavish him with the unselfish devotion to which this breed of dog so warmly responds. For many people, the purchase of a puppy is not far different from the adoption of a child. Reliable and stable temperament is a prime factor along with good health, strong bones and balanced structure. The Great Dane is easily housebroken, nearly odorless, rarely barks (unless there's a good reason) and, though reserved toward strangers, is highly affectionate and loyal to his family.

STANDARDS OF THE BREED

The standards which have been adopted by the Great Dane Club of America and approved by the American Kennel Club set the present-day ideal for which Great Dane breeders are aiming. It is by these standards that the dog is judged in the show ring. However, even the most perfect specimen falls short of the standards in some respect. It's also impossible, even for a breeder or veterinarian, to tell how a puppy will shape up as an adult dog. The chances are that he will inherit the qualities for which his father and mother—or sire and dam in dog language—were bred, and if both his parents and grandparents had good show records he may have excellent possibilities.

Here, then, are the standards.

1. GENERAL CONFORMATION .... 30 points

(a) *General Appearance* (10 points)—The Great Dane combines in its distinguished appearance dignity, strength and elegance with great size and a powerful, well-formed, smoothly muscled body. He is one of the giant breeds, but is unique in that his general conformation must be so well-balanced that he never appears clumsy and is always a unit—the Apollo of dogs. He must be spirited and courageous—never timid. He is friendly and dependable. This physical and mental combination is the characteristic which gives the Great Dane the majesty possessed by no other breed. It is particularly true of this breed that there is an impression of great masculinity in males as compared to an impression of femininity in females. The male should appear more massive throughout than the female, with larger frame and heavier bone. In the ratio between length and height, the Great Dane should appear as square as possible. In females, a somewhat longer body is permissible.

Faults: Lack of unity; timidity; males with female traits; poor musculature; poor bone development; out of condition; rickets; females with male traits.

(*b*) *Color and Markings* (8 points):

1. Color: Brindle Danes. Base color ranging from light golden yellow to deep golden yellow always brindled with strong black cross stripes. The more intensive the base color and the more intensive the brindling, the more attractive will be the color. Small white marks at the chest and toes are not desirable.

Faults: Brindle with too dark a base color; silver-blue and grayish-blue base color; dull (faded) brindling; white tail tip.

2. Fawn Danes. Golden yellow up to deep golden yellow color with a deep black mask. The golden deep-yellow color must always be given the preference. Small white spots at the chest and toes are not desirable.

Faults: Yellowish-gray, bluish-yellow, grayish-blue, dirty yellow color (drab color), lack of black mask.

3. Blue Danes. The color must be a pure steel blue as far as possible without any tinge of yellow, black or mouse gray.

Faults: Any deviation from a pure steel-blue coloration.

4. Black Danes. Glossy black.

Faults: Yellow-black, brown-black or blue-black. White markings, such as stripes on the chest, speckled chest and markings on the paws are permitted but not desirable.

5. Harlequin Danes. Base color: pure white with black torn patches irregularly and well-distributed over the entire body; pure white neck preferred. The black patches should never be large enough to give the appearance of a blanket nor so small as to give a stippled or dappled effect. (Eligible but less desirable are a few small gray spots, also pointings where instead of a pure white base with black spots there is a white base with single black hairs showing through which tend to give a salt and pepper or dirty effect.)

Faults: White base color with a few large spots; bluish-gray pointed background.

(*c*) *Size* (5 points)—The male should not be less than 30 inches at the shoulders, but it is preferable that he be 32 inches or more, providing he is well proportioned to his height. The female should not be less than 28 inches at the shoulders, but it is preferable that she be 30 inches or more, providing she is well proportioned to her height.

(*d*) *Substance* (3 points)—Substance is that sufficiency of bone and muscle which rounds out a balance with the frame.

Faults: Lightweight whippety Danes; coarse, ungainly proportioned Danes; always there should be balance.

(*e*) *Condition of Coat* (4 points)—The coat should be very short and thick, smooth and glossy.

Faults: Excessively long hair (stand-off coat); dull hair (indicating malnutrition, worms and negligent care).

(Above) This handsome golden brindle is Ch. Shalott's Sir Dorian at 14 months of age, owned by Bette Laufcheimer.

(Below) Only 9 months old, this sleek black Dane bred by the Honey Hollow Kennels looks forward to winning his championship.

2. MOVEMENT ...... 28 points

(a) *Gait* (10 points)—Long, easy, springy stride with no tossing or rolling of body. The back line should move smoothly, parallel to the ground. The gait of the Great Dane should denote strength and power. The rear legs should have drive. The forelegs should track smoothly and straight. The Dane should track in two parallel straight lines.

Faults: Short steps. The rear quarters should not pitch. The forelegs should not have a hackney gait (forced or choppy stride). When moving rapidly the Great Dane should not pace, as this causes excessive side-to-side rolling of the body and thus reduces endurance.

(b) *Rear End* (*Croup, Legs, Paws*) (10 points)—The croup must be full, slightly drooping and must continue imperceptibly to the tail root. Hind legs, the first thighs (from hip joint to knee) are broad and muscular. The second thighs (from knee to hock joint) are strong and long. Seen from the side, the angulation of the first thigh with the body, of the second thigh with the first thigh, and the pastern root with the second thigh should be very moderate, neither too straight nor too exaggerated. Seen from the rear, the hock joints appear to be perfectly straight, turned neither towards the inside nor towards the outside.

Faults: A croup which is too straight; a croup which slopes downward too steeply; and too narrow a croup. Hind legs: Soft, flabby, poorly muscled thighs; cowhocks which are the result of the hock joint turning inward and the hock and rear paws turning outward; barrel legs, the result of the hock joints being too far apart; steep rear. As seen from the side, a steep rear is the result of the angles of the rear legs forming almost a straight line; overangulation is the result of exaggerated angles between the first and second thighs and the hocks and is very conducive to weakness. The rear legs should never be too long in proportion to the front legs.

Paws, round and turned neither towards the inside nor towards the outside. Toes short, highly arched and well closed. Nails short, strong and as dark as possible.

Faults: Spreading toes (splay foot); bent, long toes (rabbit paws); toes turned towards the outside or towards the inside. Furthermore, the fifth toe on the hind legs appearing at a higher position and with wolf's claw or spur; excessively long nails; light-colored nails.

(c) *Front End* (*Shoulders, Legs, Paws*) (8 points)—*Shoulders:* The shoulder blades must be strong and sloping and seen from the side, must form as nearly as possible a right angle in its articulation with the humerus (upper arm) to give a long stride. A line from the upper tip of the shoulder to the back of the elbow joint should be as nearly perpendicular as possible. Since all dogs lack a clavicle (collar bone) the ligaments and muscles holding the shoulder blade to the rib cage must be well developed, firm and secure to prevent loose shoulders.

Faults: Steep shoulders, which occur if the shoulder blade does not slope sufficiently; overangulation; loose shoulders which occur if the Dane is flabbily muscled, or if the elbow is turned toward the outside; loaded shoulders.

Forelegs: The upper arm should be strong and muscular. Seen from the side or front the strong lower arms run absolutely straight to the pastern joints.

Seen from the front, the forelegs and the pastern roots should form perpendicular lines to the ground. Seen from the side, the pastern root should slope only very slightly forward.

Faults: Elbows turned toward the inside or toward the outside, the former position caused mostly by too narrow or too shallow a chest, bringing the front legs too closely together and at the same time turning the entire lower part of the leg outward; the latter position causes the front legs to spread too far apart, with the pastern roots and paws usually turned inwards. Seen from the side, a considerable bend in the pastern toward the front indicates weakness and is in most cases connected with stretched and spread toes (splay foot); seen from the side a forward bow in the forearm (chair leg); an excessively knotty bulge in the front of the pastern joint.

Paws: Round and turned neither toward the inside nor toward the outside. Toes short, highly arched and well closed. Nails short, strong and as dark as possible.

Faults: Spreading toes (splay foot), bent, long toes (rabbit paws); toes turned toward the outside or toward the inside; light-colored nails.

3. HEAD .... 20 points

(a) *Head Conformation* (12 points)—Long, narrow, distinguished, expressive, finely chiseled, especially the part below the eyes (which means that the skull plane under and to the inner point of the eye must slope without any bony protuberance in a pleasing line to the full square jaw), with strong pronounced stop. The masculinity of the male is very pronounced in the expression and structure of head (this subtle difference should be evident in the dog's head through massive skull and depth of muzzle); the female's head may be more delicately formed. Seen from the side, the forehead must be sharply set off from the bridge of the nose. The forehead and the bridge of the nose must be straight and parallel to one another. Seen from the front, the head should appear narrow, the bridge of the nose should be as broad as possible. The cheek muscles must show slightly but under no circumstances should they be too pronounced (cheeky). The muzzle part must have full flews and must be as blunt vertically as possible in front; the angles of the lip must be quite pronounced. The front part of the head, from the tip of the nose up to the center of the stop should be as long as the rear part of the head from the center of the stop to the only slightly developed occiput. The head should be angular from all sides and should have definite flat planes and its dimensions should be absolutely in proportion to the general appearance of the Dane.

Faults: Any deviation from the parallel planes of skull and foreface; too small a stop; a poorly defined stop or none at all; too narrow a nose bridge; the rear of the head spreading laterally in a wedgelike manner (wedge head); an excessively round upper head (apple head); excessively pronounced cheek musculature; pointed muzzle; loose lips hanging over the lower jaw (fluttering lips) which create an illusion of a full deep muzzle. The head should be rather shorter and distinguished than long and expressionless.

(b) *Teeth* (4 points)—Strong, well developed and clean. The incisors of the lower jaw must touch very lightly the bottoms of the inner surface of the upper

The ideal Dane head is distinguished and expressive.

incisors (scissors bite). If the front teeth of both jaws bite on top of each other, they wear down too rapidly.

Faults: Even bite; undershot and overshot; incisors out of line; black or brown teeth; missing teeth.

(*c*) *Eyes* (4 points)—Medium size, as dark as possible, with lively intelligent expression; almond-shaped eyelids, well-developed eyebrows.

Faults: Light-colored, piercing, amber-colored, light blue to a watery blue, red or bleary eyes; eyes of different colors; eyes too far apart; Mongolian eyes; eyes with pronounced haws; eyes with excessively drooping lower eyelids. In blue and black Danes, lighter eyes are permitted but are not desirable. In harlequins, the eyes should be dark. Light colored eyes, two eyes of different color and walleyes are permitted but not desirable.

Nose (0 points)—The nose must be large and in the case of brindled and "single-colored" Danes, it must always be black. In harlequins, the nose should be black; a black spotted nose is permitted; a pink-colored nose is not desirable.

Ears (0 points)—Ears should be high, set not too far apart, medium in size, of moderate thickness, drooping forward close to the cheek. Top line of folded ear should be about level with the skull.

Faults: Hanging on the side, as on a Foxhound. Cropped ears; high set: not set too far apart, well pointed but always in proportion to the shape of the head and carried uniformly erect.

4. TORSO .... 20 points

(*a*) *Neck* (6 points)—The neck should be firm and clean, high-set, well arched, long, muscular and sinewy. From the chest to the head, it should be slightly tapering, beautifully formed, with well-developed nape.

Faults: Short, heavy neck, pendulous throat folds (dewlaps).

(*b*) *Loin and Back* (6 points)—The withers form the highest part of the back which slopes downward slightly toward the loins, which are imperceptibly arched and strong. The back should be short and tensely set. The belly should be well shaped and tightly muscled, and, with the rear part of the thorax, should swing in a pleasing curve (tuck-up).

Faults: Receding back; sway back; camel or roach back; a back line which is too high at the rear; an excessively long back; poor tuck-up.

(*c*) *Chest* (4 points)—Chest deals with that part of the thorax (rib cage) in front of the shoulders and front legs. The chest should be quite broad, deep and well muscled.

Faults: A narrow and poorly muscled chest; strong protruding sternum (pigeon breast).

(*d*) *Ribs and Brisket* (4 points)—Deals with that part of the thorax back of the shoulders and front legs. Should be broad, with the ribs sprung well out from the spine and flattened at the side to allow proper movement of the shoulders extending down to the elbow joint.

Faults: Narrow (slab-sided) rib cage; round (barrel) rib cage; shallow rib cage not reaching the elbow joint.

5. TAIL .... 2 points
Should start high and fairly broad, terminating slender and thin at the hock joint. At rest, the tail should fall straight. When excited or running, slightly curved (saberlike).

Faults: A too high, or too low set tail (the tail set is governed by the slope of the croup); too long or too short a tail; tail bent too far over the back (ring tail); a tail which is curled; a twisted tail (sideways); a tail carried too high over the back (gay tail); a brush tail (hair too long on lower side). Cropping tails to desired length is forbidden.

2. Selecting Your Great Dane

Once you decide that the Great Dane is the dog for you, how do you go about choosing the right one, when you are faced with a group of Dane puppies at the kennels? (Due to its size, a Dane is seldom found in a pet shop.) Your first interest should be in obtaining a healthy animal. Try to select the one that's the most active and aggressive. If the puppies have just been fed and are sleepy, wait a while before making your selection. Check the dog's eyes and ears for any puslike discharge, and pass him over if his eyes or ears are running. A running nose or a very dry nose can also be a danger sign in a young puppy. Look at his teeth and gums and make sure they are not bleeding. If the puppy is having a bowel movement, it should not be watery.

A puppy which does not have straight legs is not a wise choice. Look for dark eyes, a long head and a deep muzzle. Check to see that he does not have a scissors bite, and avoid a pup which has an apple or domed head.

You had better bypass, too, a pup which is all white, or a harlequin which has mostly yellow, gray, blue or brindle spots. Any spots should be sharply defined, not washed out or smudged. Also, avoid a harlequin puppy with a large spot covering his body like a coat.

Whether you are in the small, medium or large financial bracket, you have a right to expect a healthy puppy and one that is free from any mental disorders. Most breeders today are experienced in the use of vitamins, minerals and calcium. Reliable Great Dane dealers furnish their puppies with plenty of red meat and high-quality dry foods.

It is always wise to make your purchase subject to the approval of a veterinarian. The seller will usually allow you eight hours in which to take the puppy to a vet to have his health checked. Arrive at a clear agreement with the seller on what happens if the vet rejects the puppy. It should be understood whether rejection means you get your money back or merely the choice of another puppy. One word of caution before you take the puppy to be examined; it sometimes happens that a veterinarian is not familiar with the rapid growth and development of the Great Dane; if this should be the case, he might diagnose the enlarged joints of a Great Dane puppy as rickets.

All purebred puppies should have an American Kennel Club registration and a pedigree for at least three generations. Ask to see copies of these, and look for the "Ch." in the listings of the dog's parents and grandparents. This denotes dogs that have won their breed championships.

Prospective buyers of Great Danes frequently ask: "What constitutes the difference between a show Great Dane and a pet?"

Although the situation is somewhat deplorable, there appears to be scarcely

This 6-week-old Harlequin puppy is just waiting to be adopted by some appreciative family.

any difference between the average show specimen and "just a pet." Actually, any Great Dane can be sold for or considered as show stock if he does not have faults that are set down as disqualifications in the official standard. Unfortunately, this gives the unethical or irresponsible breeder-seller (there are not many, but they do exist) an appallingly wide range to promote show stock.

It's going to be a hard choice when you are confronted with a litter of eager, active Dane puppies. Health and disposition should be your first considerations.

EAR-CROPPING

Most Great Dane puppies are purchased after ear-cropping, and are usually not available until two months of age. If you buy one with uncropped ears, it should not be taken from the kennels until at least six weeks of age.

Over the years there has been a lot of controversy concerning the subject of ear-cropping. On one side are the people representing the humanitarian societies. Supporting them are enthusiasts who say that any disfigurement of a dog's natural lines is in effect a dishonesty, and that if cropped-type ears are so important, a concentrated effort should be made to breed them that way.

Opposed to these views are those who say that cropping does not harm the dog but, on the contrary, removes the portion of ear that becomes torn when he gets into fights. In addition, they say, cropped ears give dogs a smarter, more racy appearance.

The standard states that Great Dane's ears may or may not be cropped, and most shows held in the half-dozen or so states in which it is illegal to crop ears will not approve of the showing of dogs with this alteration. (Some states set down exact veterinarian specifications to be followed when cropping.)

As long ago as 1895, ear-cropping was outlawed in England, so Great Danes have natural ears there. For some years after cropping was forbidden, natural

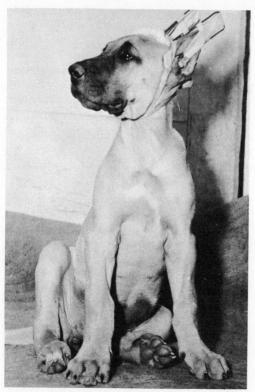

His taped and pinned-back ears don't seem to bother this inquisitive-looking pup.

ears were heavy and unpleasant to see. Since then, however, breeders have surmounted the difficulty with marked success, breeding animals with ears that are smaller, tighter and sleeker. Their accomplishment lends support to those Americans who say that ear-cropping is pure foolishness.

MALE OR FEMALE?

If you should intend breeding your dog in the future, by all means buy a female. You can find a suitable mate without difficulty when the time comes, and have the pleasure of raising a litter of pups—there is nothing cuter than a fat, playful puppy. If you don't want to raise puppies, your female can be spayed, and will remain a healthy, lively pet. The female is smaller than the male and generally quieter. She has less tendency to roam in search of romance, but a properly trained male can be a charming pet, and has a certain difference in temperament that is appealing to many people. Male vs. female is chiefly a matter of personal choice.

ADULT OR PUP?

Whether to buy a grown dog or a small puppy is another question. It is undeniably fun to watch your dog grow all the way from a baby, sprawling and playful, to a mature, dignified dog. If you don't have the time to spend on the more frequent meals, housebreaking, and other training a puppy needs in order to become a dog you can be proud of, then choose an older, partly trained pup or a grown dog. If you want a show dog, remember that no one, not even an expert, can predict with 100 per cent accuracy what a small puppy will be when he grows up.

HOW TO REGISTER YOUR GREAT DANE

As a rule, the puppy you buy has not been registered as an individual, but the breeder has probably registered the litter. Unless he has done this, you cannot register your puppy with the American Kennel Club. Both the puppy's parents must have been registered as purebred Great Danes too. An unregistered dog cannot qualify for dog show awards or for obedience degrees and its offspring will be less valuable.

To register with the A.K.C., obtain an Application for Registration from the seller who will fill in the lines on the form that transfer ownership to you. The form should also bear the signature of the owner of the dam (mother in dog-language). Then you select a name for your dog (it must be 25 letters or less, and cannot duplicate the name of another dog of the breed, or be the name of a living person without his written permission). Enter the selected name on the form, fill in the blanks that make you the owner of record, and send it to the American Kennel Club, 221 Park Avenue South, New York, New York, with the required registration fee. In a few weeks you will receive a Certificate of Registration with your dog's name (if it is approved) and registration number.

Actually, all this isn't as complicated as it may appear. It's routine with the dog seller, and the forms are no more complicated than applications for a marriage license or a personal loan.

THE PEDIGREE

The pedigree of your dog is a tracing of his family tree. Often the breeder will have the pedigree of the dog's dam and sire and may make out a copy for you. Or, you can write to the American Kennel Club once your dog has been registered and ask for a pedigree. The fee depends on how many generations back you want the pedigree traced. In addition to giving the immediate ancestors of your dog, the pedigree will show whether there are any champions or dogs that have won obedience degrees in his lineage. If you are planning selective breeding, the pedigree is also helpful to enable you to find other Great Danes that have the same general family background.

WORMING AND INOCULATION

Before you take your puppy home, find out from the breeder if he has already been wormed or inoculated for distemper and rabies. Practically all puppies will have worms, which they acquire from eating worm eggs, from fleas, or from their mother. The breeder usually gives the puppies a worming before he sells them. If yours has already been wormed, find out when and what treatment was given. The breeder may be able to advise you on any further treatment that is necessary. While there are many commercial worming preparations on the market, it's generally safer to let the vet handle it. There will be more about worms in Chapter 3.

If your puppy has been inoculated against distemper, you will also have to know when this was done so you can give the information to your vet. He will complete the series of shots. If your puppy has not yet been given this protection, your vet should take care of it immediately. Distemper is highly prevalent and contagious. Don't let your puppy out of doors until he has had his distemper shots and they have had time to take effect.

As a rule, kennels and breeders do not inoculate puppies against rabies. In some areas, rabies inoculation is required by law. However, the possibility of your dog's becoming affected with rabies, a contact disease, is very slight in most parts of the country. To be perfectly safe, check with your vet who will be familiar with the local ordinances and will advise you.

While the distemper inoculation is permanent and can be supplemented by "booster" shots, rabies inoculation must be repeated yearly. When your puppy receives it, the vet will give you a tag for the dog's collar certifying that he has received the protection. He will also give you a certificate for your own records. For foreign travel and some interstate travel, rabies inoculation is required.

3. Caring for Your Great Dane

BRINGING YOUR PUPPY HOME

When you bring your puppy home, remember that he is used to the peace and relative calm of a life of sleeping, eating and playing with his brothers and sisters. The trip away from all this is an adventure in itself, and so is adapting to a new home. So let him take it easy for a while. Don't let the whole neighborhood pat and poke him at one time. Be particularly careful when children want to handle him, for they cannot understand the difference between the delicate living puppy and the toy dog they play with and maul. Show them the correct way to hold the puppy, supporting his belly with one hand while holding him securely with the other.

THE PUPPY'S BED

It is up to you to decide where the puppy will sleep. He should have his own place, and not be allowed to climb all over the furniture. He should sleep out of drafts, but not right next to the heat, which would make him too sensitive to the cold when he goes outside.

A Great Dane puppy is a little too large to grow up in a box. You might partition off a section of a room—the kitchen is good because it's usually warm and he'll have some companionship there. Set up some sort of partition that he can't climb, give him a pillow or old blanket for his bed and cover the floor with a thick layer of newspapers.

Don't make the mistake of buying a bed or even a sleeping pad for a young puppy. He's certain to demolish it. You might buy some cedar shavings and make a "nest" of them. They help prevent a doggy odor and may discourage fleas.

You have already decided where the puppy will sleep before you bring him home. Let him stay there, or in the corner he will soon learn is "his," most of the time, so that he will gain a sense of security from the familiar. Give the puppy a little food when he arrives, but don't worry if he isn't hungry at first. He will soon develop an appetite when he grows accustomed to his surroundings. The first night the puppy may cry a bit from lonesomeness, but if he has an old blanket or rug to curl up in he will be cozy. In winter a hot water bottle will help replace the warmth of his littermates, or the ticking of a clock may provide company.

SUGGESTED DIET

Always find out what the breeder has been feeding your puppy as it is well to keep him on the same food for a while. Any sudden change may cause an upset stomach.

Attentive and affectionate care, a well-balanced diet and enough exercise provide the surest guarantee that your puppy will grow up to be a healthy and happy dog. This 3-month-old fawn trio was sired by Ch. Honey Hollow Stormi Rudio, acknowledged to be one of the all-time top winners in the show ring.

A puppy that is five to six weeks of age should be fed not less than four times a day. Give him two level tablespoons of puréed meat—fresh, lean chopped beef put through a mixer until it is creamy smooth like peanut butter—two tablespoons of condensed milk diluted with two tablespoons of hot water and two tablespoons of Pablum. Add two to three drops of a high-potency cod-liver oil plus one teaspoon of a multiple vitamin powder (preferably one recommended by the breeder or a veterinarian) to his food.

Gradually replace the puréed beef with ground beef (fatty), a good brand of puppy meal or kibble and continue with the canned milk. Gradually increase amounts of cod-liver oil and vitamin powder, and decrease to three meals each day.

Gauging the amounts of beef and kibble depends on the size and appetite of the puppy. When he is two to three months of age, give him approximately $\frac{1}{4}$ to $\frac{1}{2}$ pound of beef to $\frac{1}{2}$ to one cup of kibble, mixed with $\frac{1}{2}$ cup of milk and $\frac{1}{2}$ cup of hot water, three times per day.

Even a full-grown Great Dane won't break you financially, as he doesn't eat more than most of the larger breeds. From four months of age through adulthood, he should be fed plenty of fresh meat, preferably beef. If you use horsemeat, tripe or a non-fatty beef substitute, add some chopped beef suet. A Great Dane requires more fat and starch in his diet than terriers and many other breeds. It is advisable to feed him twice a day, rather than once.

According to size, weight and appetite, a Great Dane requires from one to 3 pounds of meat each day (in two meals) and 4, 6 or 8 cups of kibble biscuit or meal (in two meals), mixed with enough hot water to dampen and expand the kibble or meal. Most Great Danes like their food on the dry side rather than soupy. Season with iodized salt.

It is advisable also occasionally to substitute cooked rice, noodles, macaroni and spaghetti for the prepared dry kibble foods. Many breeders keep their Great Danes in excellent condition by feeding them hard-crusted breads (white or dark).

In addition to his daily diet, a Great Dane (of any age) should have a high-potency multiple-vitamin capsule each day.

Be sure that your dog always has a good supply of cool, fresh, clean water available.

Many canine periodicals deplore the practice of feeding dogs table scraps or tidbits. A Great Dane, however, is a "people dog" and he enjoys and thrives on a "people diet." There is nothing that he enjoys more than a generous handout from the table. Cooked vegetables, gravies, potatoes, chicken, lamb, steak, turkey and boneless fish can supplement his basic daily diet, but don't give him pork products or shellfish. Great Danes love ice cream and milk shakes. One famous champion relished scrambled eggs, any variety of cheese, and corn muffins garnished with steak bits and roast beef. This dog kept in superb condition and won many Bests-in-Show. Many Great Danes also like raw vegetables and fruits. And like horses, they adore lump sugar.

While your dog can eat almost everything you can, there are some foods you should avoid. Be especially careful with chicken or fish bones, which might lodge in his throat or cause intestinal trouble.

Don't worry if he skips an occasional meal. If he isn't interested in eating, take the food away after 10 or 15 minutes. A number of kennels purposely eliminate one meal a week, feeling that it makes the dogs more active and alert. Many exhibitors do not feed their dogs the day of a show. Use your own judgment about that.

Common sense is the most important factor in feeding a puppy or young dog. If your dog looks thin, he probably needs more food; if he is heavy after he outgrows his puppy fat, he may be overfed. If you find that some foods give him loose bowels or gas, change his menu. However, if you think you are feeding him properly and he isn't responding the way you think he should be, a trip to the vet might be advisable.

WATCHING THE PUPPY'S HEALTH

The first step in protecting the health of your puppy is a visit to the veterinarian. If the breeder has not given your puppy his first distemper shots, have your vet do it. You should also have your dog protected against hepatitis, and, if required by local law or if your vet suggests it, against rabies. Your puppy should receive his full quota of protective inoculations, especially if you plan to show him later. Select a veterinarian you feel you can trust and keep his phone number handy. Any vet will be glad to give a regular "patient" advice over the phone—often without charge.

Occasional loose bowels in a puppy generally isn't anything too serious. It can be the result of an upset stomach or a slight cold. Sometimes it will clear up in a day or so without any treatment. If you want to help the puppy's digestion, add some cottage cheese to his diet, or give him a few drops of kaopectate. Instead of tap water, give him barley or oatmeal water (just as you would a human baby). However, if the looseness persists for more than a day or two, a visit to the vet may be required. If the puppy has normal bowel

There may come a time when you have to give your dog medicine. Instead of a dropper, which he may break, use a spoon. Pour the medicine into his mouth and hold his head back and mouth closed until he swallows.

movements alternating with loose bowel movements, it may be a symptom of worms.

If the puppy upchucks a meal or vomits up slime or white froth, it may indicate that his stomach is upset. One good stomach-settler is a pinch of baking soda, or about 8 or 10 drops of pure witch hazel in a teaspoon of cold water two or three times a day. In case of vomiting you should skip a few meals to give the stomach a chance to clear itself out. When you start to feed him again, give him cooked scraped beef for his first meals and then return to his normal diet. Persistent vomiting may indicate a serious stomach upset or even poisoning and calls for professional help.

WORMING

Practically all puppies start out in life with worms in their insides, either acquired from the mother or picked up in their sleeping quarters. However, there are six different types of worms. Some will be visible in the stool as small white objects; others require microscopic examination of the stool for identification. While there are many commercial worm remedies on the market, it is safest to leave that to your veterinarian, and to follow his instructions on feeding the puppy before and after the worming. If you find that you must administer a worm remedy yourself, read the directions carefully and administer the smallest possible dose. Keep the puppy confined after treatment for worms, since many of the remedies have a strong laxative action and the puppy will soil the house if allowed to roam freely.

THE USEFUL THERMOMETER

Almost every serious puppy ailment shows itself by an increase in the puppy's body temperature. If your Great Dane acts lifeless, looks dull-eyed and gives an impression of illness, check by using a rectal thermometer. Hold the dog, insert the thermometer which has been lubricated with vaseline and take a reading. The normal temperature is 100.6 to 101.5 (higher than the normal human temperature). Excitement may send it up slightly, but any rise of more than a few points is cause for alarm.

To weigh your dog, first weigh yourself. Then get on the scale again, this time holding your pet (it won't be easy when he grows up!) Subtract your weight alone from yours and the dog's together to get his weight.

SOME CANINE DISEASES

Amateur diagnosis is dangerous because the symptoms of so many dog diseases are alike, but you should be familiar with most of the diseases which can strike your dog.

COUGHS, COLDS, BRONCHITIS, PNEUMONIA

Respiratory diseases may affect the dog because he is forced to live in a human rather than a natural doggy environment. Being subjected to a draft or cold after a bath, sleeping near an air conditioner or in the path of air from a fan or near a hot air register or radiator can cause one of these respiratory ailments. The symptoms are similar to those in humans. However, the germs of these diseases are different and do not affect both dogs and humans so that they cannot catch them from each other. Treatment is pretty much the same as for a child with the same illness. Keep the puppy warm, quiet, well fed. Your veterinarian has antibiotics and other remedies to help the pup fight back.

If your puppy gets wet, dry him immediately to guard against chilling. Wipe his stomach after he has walked through damp grass. Don't make the common mistake of running your dog to the vet every time he sneezes. If he seems to have a light cold, give him about a quarter of an aspirin tablet and see that he doesn't overexercise.

MAJOR DISEASES OF THE DOG

With the proper series of inoculations, your Great Dane will be almost completely protected against the following canine diseases. However, it occasionally happens that the shot doesn't take and sometimes a different form of the virus appears, against which your dog may not be protected.

Rabies: This is an acute disease of the dog's central nervous system and is spread by the bite of an infected animal, the saliva carrying the infection. Rabies occurs in two forms. The first is "Furious Rabies" in which the dog shows a period of melancholy or depression, then irritation, and finally paralysis. The first period lasts from a few hours to several days. During this time the dog is cross and will try to hide from members of the family. He appears restless and will change his position often. He loses his appetite for food and begins to lick, bite and swallow foreign objects. During the "irritation" phase the dog is spasmodically wild and has impulses to run away. He acts in a fearless manner and runs and bites at everything in sight. If he is caged or confined he will fight at the bars, often breaking teeth or fracturing his jaw. His bark becomes a peculiar howl. In the final or paralysis stage, the animal's lower jaw becomes paralyzed and hangs down; he walks with a stagger and saliva drips from his mouth. Within four to eight days after the onset of paralysis, the dog dies.

The second form of rabies, "Dumb Rabies," is characterized by the dog's walking in a bear-like manner with his head down. The lower jaw is paralyzed and the dog is unable to bite. Outwardly it may seem as though he has a bone caught in his throat.

Even if your pet should be bitten by a rabid dog or other animal, he can

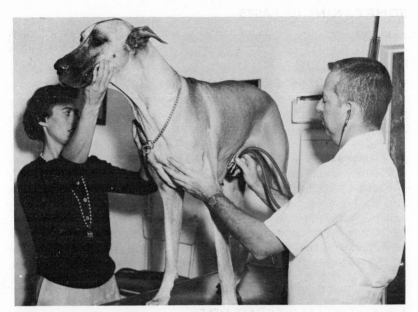

Next to you, your Great Dane has no better friend than the vet. The Dane is a sturdy breed, but you should be aware of the symptoms of the different diseases that affect dogs and know when professional help is called for.

probably be saved if you get him to the vet in time for a series of injections. However, by the time the symptoms appear the disease is so far advanced that no cure is possible. But remember that an annual rabies inoculation is almost certain protection against rabies.

Distemper: Young dogs are most susceptible to distemper, although it may affect dogs of all ages. The dog will lose his appetite, seem depressed, chilled, and run a fever. Often he will have a watery discharge from his eyes and nose. Unless treated promptly, the disease goes into advanced stages with infections of the lungs, intestines and nervous system, and dogs that recover may be left with some impairment such as a twitch or other nervous mannerism. The best protection against this is very early inoculation—preferably even before the puppy is old enough to go out into the street and meet other dogs.

Hepatitis: Veterinarians report an increase in the spread of this virus disease in recent years, usually with younger dogs as the victims. The initial symptoms— drowsiness, vomiting, great thirst, loss of appetite and a high temperature— closely resemble distemper. These symptoms are often accompanied by swellings on the head, neck and lower parts of the belly. The disease strikes quickly and death may occur in a few hours. Protection is afforded by injection with a new vaccine.

Leptospirosis: This disease is caused by bacteria which live in stagnant or slow-moving water. It is carried by rats and dogs, and many dogs are believed to get it from licking the urine or feces of infected rats. The symptoms are

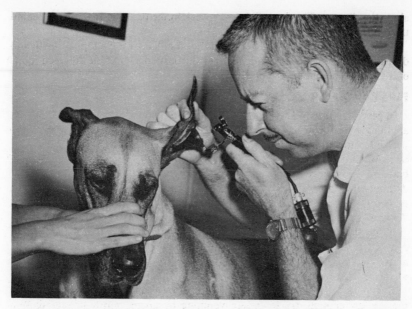

A thorough examination, plus protective inoculations, will safeguard your dog's health.

increased thirst, depression and weakness. In the acute stage, there is vomiting, diarrhea and a brown discoloration of the jaws, tongue and teeth, caused by an inflammation of the kidneys. This disease can be cured if caught in time, but it is best to ward it off with a vaccine which your vet can administer along with the distemper shots.

External Parasites: The dog that is groomed regularly and provided with clean sleeping quarters should not be troubled with fleas, ticks or lice. However, it would be a wise precaution to spray his sleeping quarters occasionally with an anti-parasite powder that you can get at your pet shop or from your vet. If the dog is out of doors during the tick season he should be treated with a dip-bath.

Skin Ailments: Any persistent scratching may indicate an irritation, and whenever you groom your dog, look for the reddish spots that may indicate eczema or some rash or fungus infection. Do not treat him yourself. Take him to the veterinarian as some of the conditions may be difficult to eradicate and can cause permanent harm to his coat.

Rickets: Occasionally, due to some internal deficiencies or imbalance of his body's metabolism, a well-fed dog does not properly assimilate his food, calcium or supplements and will develop a bad case of rickets. If this happens, the dog should be taken to a vet who will determine the cause and remedy.

Rickets in Great Danes can be determined by crooked and/or bowed legs. The vertebrae will not be straight and bumps that resemble a rosary will appear along the rib cage. The dog will be very weak in the pasterns or the skull behind the eyes will be sunken.

Remember, however, that a vet who is not familiar with the rapid growth and development of the Great Dane might erroneously diagnose the enlarged joints of a Great Dane puppy as rickets.

FIRST AID FOR YOUR DOG

In general, a dog will lick his cuts and wounds and they'll heal. If he swallows anything harmful, chances are he'll throw it up. But it will probably make you feel better to help him if he's hurt, so treat his wounds as you would your own. Wash out the dirt and apply an antiseptic or ointment. If you put on a bandage, you'll have to do something to keep the dog from trying to remove it. A large cardboard ruff around his neck will prevent him from licking his chest or body. You can tape up his nails to keep him from scratching, or make a "bootie" for his paws.

If you think your dog has a broken bone, before moving him apply a splint just as you would to a person's limb. If there is bleeding that won't stop, apply a tourniquet between the wound and heart, but loosen it every few minutes to prevent damage to the circulatory system.

If you are afraid that your dog has swallowed poison and you can't get the vet fast enough, try to induce vomiting by giving him a strong solution of salt water or mustard in water.

SOME "BUTS"

First, don't be frightened by the number of diseases a dog can get. The majority of dogs never get any of them. If you need assurance, look at any book on human diseases. How many have you had?

Don't become a dog-hypochondriac. Veterinarians have enough work taking care of sick dogs and doing preventive work with their patients. Don't rush your pet to the vet every time he sneezes or seems tired. All dogs have days on which they feel lazy and want to lie around doing nothing.

THE FEMALE PUPPY

If you want to spay your female you can have it done while she is still a puppy. Her first seasonal period will probably occur between eight and ten months, although it may be as early as six or delayed until she is a year old. She may be spayed before or after this, or you may breed her (at a later season) and still spay her afterward.

The first sign of the female's being in season is a thin red discharge, which will increase for about a week, when it changes color to a thin yellowish stain, lasting about another week. Simultaneously there is a swelling of the vulva, the dog's external sexual organ. The second week is the crucial period, when she could be bred if you wanted her to have puppies, but it is possible for the period to be shorter or longer, so it is best not to take unnecessary risks at any time. After a third week the swelling decreases and the period is over for about six months.

If you have an absolutely climb-proof and dig-proof run within your yard, it will be safe to leave her there, but otherwise the female in season should be shut indoors. Don't leave her out alone for even a minute; she should be exercised only on leash. If you want to prevent the neighborhood dogs from hanging around your doorstep, as they inevitably will as soon as they discover that your female is in season, take her some distance away from the house before you let her relieve herself. Take her in the car to a nearby park or field for a chance to stretch her legs. After the three weeks are up you can let her out as before, with no worry that she can have puppies until the next season. But if you want to have her spayed, consult your veterinarian about the time and age at which he prefers to do it. With a young dog the operation is simple and after a night or two at the animal hospital she can be at home, wearing only a small bandage as a souvenir.

GROOMING THE GREAT DANE

Fortunately, the short-haired Great Dane needs little grooming. However, from puppyhood on you should accustom him to being handled. It will make trips to the vet much easier and, if you plan to show him, will prepare him for the judge's inspection.

Teach him to jump up on a low platform or bench for his grooming. While he will probably keep himself clean for the most part, you will have a really sleek-looking dog if you allow 10 or 15 minutes a day for a grooming session. At your pet shop or kennel purchase a grooming brush with fairly stiff bristles.

If you begin to groom your pet while he's still very young, he will come to enjoy it and look forward to the regular grooming sessions. While he's small, teach him to jump on a low bench so you won't have to bend over when you brush him.

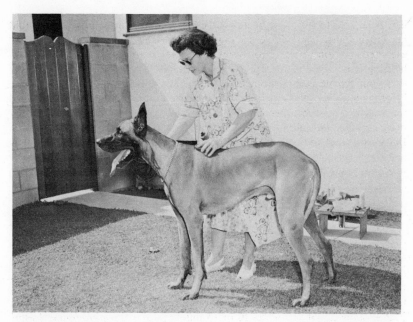

Once your Great Dane attains his full size, you won't have to do much bending. A thorough but gentle brushing will remove loose hairs and give your Dane's coat the sleek appearance that is so attractive.

When you brush your dog, brush down toward his back, and do it vigorously. The purpose of the brushing is not just to improve his appearance but to remove dirt from the hairs and skin and any dead hairs. At the same time you may brush away flea eggs and other parasites. During the summer months examine him carefully for any ticks that may be adhering to his skin. If you find ticks, you must be sure to remove the entire insects. You can touch them with a drop of iodine or a lighted cigarette (be careful not to burn the dog) to break their grip. Then lift them off, one at a time, with a pair of tweezers or a tissue and burn them or drop them into kerosene or gasoline to kill them.

BATHING YOUR DOG

Many clean-odored, shiny-coated Great Danes have never had a bath. Unless your dog gets into something that just must be washed out of his coat, there is little reason to bathe him. The Saturday night bath is an institution that was never meant to apply to the dog. Frequent bathing will ruin his coat and dry out his skin. If you do feel the need to bathe your dog, use one of the dog soaps with a high oil content. Wash toward the tail so any parasites may be removed. As a precaution, put some cotton into his ears and a few drops of castor oil into his eyes before bathing, to protect them from soap. Rinse him thoroughly with clear water to remove all traces of soap and dry him very carefully. Wrap him in an old towel or use an electric hair dryer and—especially in winter—keep him indoors and out of drafts until he is thoroughly dry.

(Above) Bathe your Great Dane only if he gets so dirty that there is no alternative. Use a special dog soap and be sure to rinse it all out afterward.

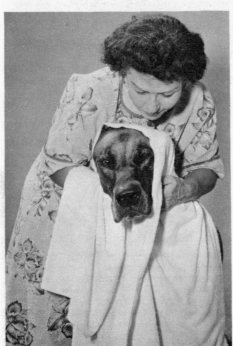

(Left) Dry your pet thoroughly after his bath to prevent chills.

Despite the great size and strength of your Great Dane, he is completely dependent on you for his comfort and well-being. Don't let him down.

There are several dry baths on the market that will do a good cleaning job on your dog and will deter or kill fleas or other parasites. You might want to check with your vet before using any of these, as some dogs may develop an allergic reaction to certain chemicals.

A GROOMING TRICK

When preparing a Great Dane for the show ring, some groomers rub their hands over the dog's coat. The oil from the palm of the human hand imparts a bright sheen to the Dane's coat.

WATCH THE TOENAILS

Many dogs that run on gravel or pavements keep their toenails down, so they seldom need clipping, But a dog that doesn't do much running, or runs on grass, will grow long toenails that can be harmful. The long nails will force the dog's toes into the air and spread his feet wide. In addition, the nails may force the dog into an unnatural stance that may produce lameness.

You can control your dog's toenails by cutting them with a special dog

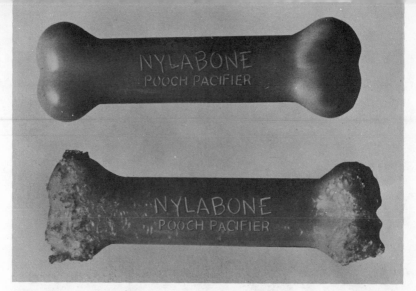

NYLABONE® is a necessity that is available at your local petshop (not in supermarkets). The puppy or grown dog chews the hambone flavored nylon into a frilly dog toothbrush, massaging his gums and cleaning his teeth as he plays. Veterinarians highly recommend this product . . . but beware of cheap imitations which might splinter or break.

clipper or by filing them. Many dogs object to the clipping and it takes some experience to learn just how to do it without cutting into the blood vessels. Your vet will probably examine your dog's nails whenever you bring him in and will trim them at no extra charge. He can show you how to do it yourself in the future. If you prefer, you can file the points off your dog's nails every few weeks with a flat wooden file.

CHECK THE EARS AND TEETH

If your Great Dane scratches at his ears or shakes his head, probe his ears very cautiously with a cotton swab dipped in mineral or castor oil. You may find an accumulation of wax that will work itself out. Any signs of dirt or dried blood in the ears probably indicates ear mites or an infection and requires treatment by your vet. In the summer, especially when flies are heavy, the dog may have sore ears from fly bites. If that happens, wash his ears with warm water and a mild soap, cover with a mild ointment and try to keep him indoors until his ears have healed.

If you give your Great Dane a hard chewing bone—the kind you can buy at a pet store—it will serve him as your toothbrush serves you and will prevent the accumulation of tartar on his teeth. However, check his mouth occasionally and take him to the vet if you find collected tartar or bloody spots on his gums.

EXERCISE

Your Great Dane will adapt himself to your way of life. If you lead a quiet life with no exercise, so will your dog, but it won't be healthy for him. In fact, it may shorten his life. If you have a fenced-in yard where he can run around, fine. If not, long walks, even on a lead, will serve just as well.

4. Housebreaking and Training Your Great Dane

The first months of your puppy's life will be a busy time. While he's getting his preventive shots and becoming acquainted with his new family, he should learn the elements of housebreaking that will make him a welcome addition to your home and community.

HOUSEBREAKING THE GREAT DANE PUPPY

Housebreaking the puppy isn't difficult because his natural instinct is to keep the place where he sleeps and plays clean. The most important factor is to keep him confined to a fairly small area during the training period. You will find it almost impossible to housebreak a puppy who is given free run of the house. After months of yelling and screaming, you may finally get it through his head that the parlor rug is "verboten," but it will be a long, arduous process.

FIRST, PAPER TRAINING

Spread papers over the puppy's living area. Then watch him carefully. When you notice him starting to whimper, sniff the floor or run around in agitated little circles, rush him to the place that you want to serve as his "toilet" and hold him there till he does his business. Then praise him lavishly. When you removed the soiled papers, leave a small damp piece so that the puppy's sense of smell will lead him back there next time. If he makes a mistake, wash it immediately with warm water, followed by a rinse with water and vinegar. That will kill the odor and prevent discoloration.

It shouldn't take more than a few days for the puppy to get the idea of using newspaper. When he becomes fairly consistent, reduce the area of paper to a few sheets in a corner. As soon as you think he has the idea fixed in his mind, you can let him roam around the house a bit, but keep an eye on him. It might be best to keep him on leash the first few days so you can rush him back to his paper at any signs of an approaching accident.

The normally healthy puppy will want to relieve himself when he wakes up in the morning, after each feeding and after strenuous exercise. During early puppyhood any excitement, such as the return home of a member of the family or the approach of a visitor, may result in floor-wetting, but that phase should pass in a few weeks.

OUTDOOR HOUSEBREAKING

Keep in mind during the housebreaking process that you can't expect

Housebreaking won't be a chore if you cover the puppy's area with papers and praise him lavishly when he uses them.

too much from your puppy until he is about 5 months old. Before that, his muscles and digestive system just aren't under his control. However, you can begin outdoor training even while you are paper training the puppy. (He should have learned to walk on lead at this point. See page 43). First thing in the morning, take him outdoors (to the curb if you are in a city) and walk him back and forth in a small area until he relieves himself. He will probably make a puddle and then just walk around uncertain of what is expected of him. You can try standing him over a piece of newspaper which may give him the idea. Some dog trainers use glycerine suppositories at this point for fast action. Praise the dog every time taking him outside brings results and he'll get the idea. After each meal take him to the same spot.

Use some training word to help your puppy learn. Pick a word that you won't use for any other command and repeat it while you are walking your dog in his outdoor "business" area. It will be a big help when the dog is older

Your Great Dane puppy will repay your love and patience with loyalty and obedience. Remember that all training takes time, and temper your discipline with plenty of affection.

if you have some word of command that he can connect with approval to relieve himself in a strange place. You'll find, when you begin the outdoor training, that the male puppy usually requires a longer walk than the female. Both male and female puppies will squat. It isn't until he's quite a bit older that the male dog will begin to lift his leg.

NIGHTTIME TRAINING

If you hate to give up any sleep, you can train your Great Dane puppy to go outdoors during the day and use the paper at night for the first few months. After he's older, he'll be able to contain himself all night and wait for his first morning walk. However, if you want to speed up the outdoor training so that you can leave the dog alone in the house with less fear of an accident, attach his leash at night so that he has enough room to move around in his bed but not enough to get any distance away from it. When he has to go, he'll whine loudly enough to attract your attention. Then take him or let him out. You may have to get up once or twice a night for a few weeks but then you can be fairly sure that your puppy will behave indoors—although accidents will happen. Sometimes even a grown dog will suddenly—and for no apparent reason—soil the house, usually the most expensive carpet in it.

Occasionally a puppy that seems to have been housebroken will revert to indiscriminate acts all over the place. If that happens it may be necessary to go back to the beginning and repeat the paper training.

WHEN HE MISBEHAVES

Rubbing a puppy's nose in his dirt or whacking him with a newspaper may make you feel better, but it won't help train the puppy. A dog naturally *wants* to do the right thing for his master. Your job is to show him what you want. If an accident happens, ignore it unless you can catch him immediately and then in a firm tone express your displeasure and take him to the spot he should have used. When he does use the right place, be lavish with praise and petting, but first be sure he has finished. Many a puppy has left a trail of water across a floor because someone interrupted him to tell him how well he was doing.

PUPPY DISCIPLINE

A 6- or 8-week-old puppy is old enough to understand what is probably the most important word in his vocabulary—"NO!" The first time you see the puppy doing something he shouldn't do, chewing something he shouldn't

An essential part of your dog's training is to keep him from approaching vehicles. If firm words do not do the trick, have a friend seated in the car beside you squirt him with a water pistol as you drive by.

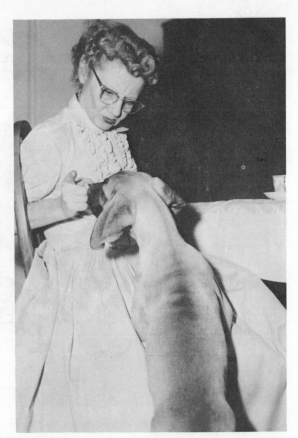

Begging for food may seem cute, but the puppy should learn what "no" means. If he is fed regularly in the same place, and if you don't allow him to beg, he won't bother you at mealtime.

chew or wandering in a forbidden area, it's time to teach him. Shout "No" and stamp your foot, hit the table with a piece of newspaper or make some other loud noise. Dogs, especially very young ones, don't like loud noises and your misbehaving pet will readily connect the word with something unpleasant. If he persists, repeat the "No," hold him firmly and slap him sharply across the nose. Before you protest to the A.S.P.C.A. you should realize that a dog does not resent being disciplined if he is doing something wrong and is caught in the act. However, do not chase a puppy around while waving a rolled-up newspaper at him or trying to swat him. Punish him only when you have a firm hold on him. Above all, never call him to you and then punish him. He must learn to associate coming to you with something pleasant.

Every puppy will pick things up. So the second command should be "Drop it!" or "Let go!" Don't engage in a tug-of-war with the puppy, but take the forbidden object from him even if you have to pry his jaws open with your fingers. Many dogs will release what they are holding if you just blow sharply into their faces. Let your dog know that you are displeased when he picks up something he shouldn't.

Fighting like cats and dogs? These two don't know the meaning of the words. If you have more than one pet, be sure to give them equal attention so neither gets jealous.

If you give him toys of his own, he will be less likely to chew your possessions. Avoid soft rubber toys that he can chew to pieces. A firm rubber ball or a tennis ball or a strong piece of leather is a good plaything. Don't give him cloth toys, either, as he'll probably swallow pieces and have trouble getting them out of his system. Skip the temptation to give him an old slipper, because it will be hard for him to distinguish between that and a brand-new pair you certainly won't want him to chew.

However, even with training, reconcile yourself to the fact that during puppy-hood things will be chewed and damaged, but that's a passing phase in the growth of the dog.

THE NOISY PUPPY

If your Great Dane is to be kept in an apartment or alone in a house for long periods, you should start an anti-noise campaign early in puppyhood. Curbing a dog's natural instinct to complain when he's left alone is most easily accomplished when he's young. You'll soon learn the difference between the sound the dog makes when he has to go out or wants food or water and the angry, complaining sound that means temper. Use the loud "No" to show him that you won't tolerate noise. Take hold of his muzzle with both hands and tell him to be quiet.

Use psychology on the dog that howls when he is left alone. Walk out of the room and close the door loudly. Then wait until you hear him making noises. When you do, pound on the door with your hand and command him to keep quiet. Walk back into the room and make sure he stops. Try this a few times. When he finds that noises from him lead to door-pounding and then severe correction from you, he'll quiet down.

However, if you want to have your Great Dane act as a watchdog, you'll have to use the opposite approach. When he makes his first puppy growls at a footstep outside or at the approach of a stranger, praise and encourage him.

JUMPING ON PEOPLE

A dog that likes people shows his affection for the human race by jumping on them. That may be cute when it's done by a tiny dog, but a full-grown Great Dane that jumps up on your friends can be just a bit of a social hazard. The cure is fairly simple if you act to nip this habit early. When your dog jumps on people, ask them to lift their knees and send him flying back. After a few lessons of that type, he'll develop a more restrained greeting. Another method is to grab the dog's front paws and flip him backward.

CLIMBING ON FURNITURE

If your Great Dane shows a fondness for climbing on furniture, this is another habit you'll have to break early. The upholstery holds the scent of the people he likes, and besides, it's more comfortable than the hard floor or even the carpet. Sometimes verbal corrections will be enough to establish the fact that the furniture is taboo. If not, try putting crinkly cellophane on the furniture to keep him off. If that doesn't work, you can get liquids at your pet store that you can't smell, but whose odor keeps the dog off.

5. Obedience Training for Your Great Dane

The purpose of obedience training is not to turn your dog into a puppet but to make him a civilized member of the community in which he will live, and to keep him safe. This training is most important as it makes the difference between having an undisciplined animal in the house or having an enjoyable companion. Both you and your dog will learn a lot from training.

HOW A DOG LEARNS

The dog is the one domestic animal that seems to want to do what his master asks. Unlike other animals that learn by fear or rewards, the dog will work willingly if he is given a kind word or a show of affection.

The hardest part of dog training is communication. If you can get across to the dog what you want him to do, he'll do it. Always remember that your dog does not understand the English language. He can, however, interpret your tone of voice and your gestures. By associating certain words with the act that accompanies them, the dog can acquire a fairly large working vocabulary. Keep in mind that it is the sound rather than the meaning of the words that the dog understands. When he doesn't respond properly, let him know by the tone of your voice that you are disappointed, but follow each correction with a show of affection.

YOUR PART IN TRAINING

You must patiently demonstrate to your dog what each simple word of command means. Guide him with your hands and the training leash through whatever routine you are teaching him. Repeat the word associated with the act. Demonstrate again and again to give the dog the chance to make the connection in his mind. (In psychological language, you are conditioning him to give a specific response to a specific stimulus.)

Once he begins to get the idea, use the word of command without any physical guidance. Drill him. When he makes mistakes, correct him, kindly at first, more severely as his training progresses. Try not to lose your patience or become irritated, and never slap him with your hand or the leash during a training session. Withholding praise or rebuking him will make him feel badly enough.

When he does what you want, praise him lavishly with words and with pats. Don't rely on dog candy or treats in training. The dog that gets into the habit of performing for treats will seldom be fully dependable when he can't smell or see one in the offing. When he carries out a command, even though his performance is slow or sloppy, praise him and he will perform more readily the next time.

THE TRAINING VOICE

When you start training your Great Dane, use your training voice, giving commands in a firm, clear tone. Once you give the command, persist until it is obeyed even if you have to pull the dog protestingly to obey you. He must learn that training is different from playing, that a command once given must be obeyed no matter what distractions are present. Remember that the tone and sound of your voice, not loudness, are the qualities that will influence your dog.

Be consistent in the use of words during training. Confine your commands to as few words as possible and never change them. It is best for only one person to carry on the dog's training because different people will use different words and tactics that will confuse the animal. The dog who hears "come," "get over here," "hurry up," "here, Rover," and other commands when he is wanted will become totally confused.

TAKE IT EASY

Training is hard on the dog—and on the trainer. A young dog just cannot take more than 10 minutes of training at a stretch, so limit the length of your first lessons. You'll find that you, too, will tend to become impatient when you stretch out a training session, and losing your temper won't help either of you. Before and after each lesson have a play period, but don't play during a training session. Even the youngest dog soon learns that schooling is a serious matter; fun comes afterward.

Don't spend too much time on one phase of training or the dog will become bored. And always try to end a training session on a pleasant note. If the dog doesn't seem to be getting what you are trying to show him, go back to something simpler that he can do. This way you will end every lesson with a pleasant feeling of accomplishment. Actually, in nine cases out of ten, if your dog isn't doing what you want, it's because you're not getting the idea over to him properly.

WALKING ON LEAD

"Doggy" people call the leash a "lead," so we'll use that term here. With your Great Dane, don't go in for any kind of fancy lead or collar. The best lead for training purposes is the 6-foot webbed-cloth lead, usually olive-drab in color.

As for the collar, you'll need a metal-link collar called a "choke" collar. Even though the name may sound frightening, it won't hurt your dog and it's an absolute *must* in training. It tightens when you snap the lead, eases when you relax your grip. It's important to put the collar on properly. Slide the chain around your dog's neck so that you can attach the lead to the ring at the end of the chain which passes *over*, not under, his neck.

Put the collar and lead on the puppy and let him walk around the house first with the lead dragging on the floor. This is just to let him get the feel of the strange object around his neck. But a word of caution for afterward: don't let the dog wander around with the choke collar on. If it's loose he'll lose it, and it's possible for it to catch on any projection and choke him. For his license tag and rabies tag you can get a light leather collar that fits more snugly.

The "choke collar" isn't as cruel as the name implies. Because of its restraining action, it is very useful for training and it cannot hurt your dog.

Now, here's a lesson for you. From the start, hold the lead firmly in your right hand. Keep the dog at your left side. You can use your left hand to jerk the lead when necessary to give corrections or to bring the dog closer to you. Do not *pull* on the lead. Give it a sharp snap when you want to correct the dog, and then release it. The dog cannot learn from being pulled around. He will learn when he finds that doing certain things results in a sharp jerk; doing other things allows him to walk comfortably on lead.

At first, the puppy will fight the lead. He'll probably plant all four feet or his rear end on the ground and wait for your next move. Be patient. Short tugs on the lead will help him learn his part in walking with you. If he gets overexcited, calm him before taking off the lead and collar and picking him up. He must learn there's nothing to fear. (Incidentally, if the lesson is being given on a city street, it might be a good idea to carry some paper to clean up the mess he may leave in his excitement.)

Hold the lead firmly in your right hand, using your left to make corrections when necessary.

TRAINING TO SIT

Training your dog to sit should be fairly easy. Stand him on your left side, holding the lead fairly short, and command him to "Sit." As you give the verbal command, pull up slightly with the lead and push his hindquarters down (you may have to kneel to do this). Do not let him lie down or stand up. Keep him in a sitting position for a moment, then release the pressure on the lead and praise him. Constantly repeat the command word as you hold him in a sitting position, thus fitting the word to the action in his mind. After a while, he will begin to get the idea and will sit without your having to push his back down. When he reaches that stage, insist that he sit on command. If he is slow to obey, slap his hindquarters with the end of the lead to get him down fast. Teach him to sit on command facing you as well as when he is at your side. When he begins sitting on command with the lead on, try it with the lead off.

Obedience training should begin indoors, where there are fewer distractions, but it's the training outdoors that is vital to your pet's safety. He must learn to obey you no matter what temptations are present.

THE "LIE DOWN"

The object of this is to get the dog to lie down either on the verbal command "Down!" or when you give him a hand signal, your hand raised, palm toward the dog—a sort of threatening gesture. This is one of the most important parts of training. A well-trained dog will drop on command and stay down whatever the temptation—car-chasing, cat-chasing, or another dog across the street.

Don't start this until the dog is almost letter-perfect in sitting on command. Then, place the dog in a sit. Force him down by pulling his front feet out forward while pressing on his shoulders and repeating "Down!" Hold the dog down and stroke him gently to let him know that staying down is what you expect of him.

After he begins to get the idea, slide the lead under your left foot and give the command "Down!" At the same time, pull on the lead. This will help get the dog down. Meanwhile, raise your hand in the down signal. Don't expect to accomplish all this in one session. Be patient and work with the dog. He'll cooperate if you show him just what you expect him to do.

THE "STAY"

The next step is to train your dog to stay in either a "sit" or "down" position. Sit him at your side. Give him the command "Stay," but be careful not to use his name with that command as hearing his name may lead him to think that some action is expected of him. If he begins to move, repeat "Stay" firmly and hold him down in the sit. Constantly repeat the word "stay" to fix the meaning of that command in his mind. When he stays for a short time, gradually increase the length of his stay. The hand signal for "stay" is a downward sweep of your hand toward the dog's nose, with the palm toward him. While he is sitting, walk around him and stand in front of him. Hold the lead at first; later, drop the lead on the ground in front of him and keep him sitting. If he bolts, correct him severely and force him back to a sit in the same place.

Use some word such as "okay" or "up" to let him know when he can get up, and praise him well for a good performance. As this practice continues, walk farther and farther away from him. Later, try sitting him, giving him the command to stay, and then walk out of sight, first for a few seconds, then for longer periods. A well-trained dog should stay where you put him without moving for three minutes or more.

Similarly, practice having him stay in down position, first with you near him, later when you step out of sight.

THE "COME" ON COMMAND

A young puppy will come a-running to people, but an older puppy or dog will have other plans of his own when his master calls him. However, you can

A well-trained dog will lie down on command and stay in position until you give the okay to get up.

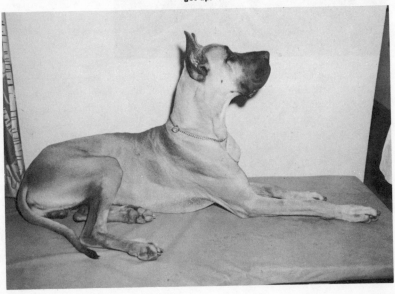

After your Dane has learned to sit facing you while on lead, try it with the lead off.

train your dog to come when you call him if you begin when he is young. At first, work with him on lead. Sit the dog, then back away the length of the lead and call him, putting as much coaxing affection in your voice as possible. Give an easy tug on the lead to get him started. When he does come, make a big fuss over him and it might help to hand him a piece of dog candy or food as a reward. He should get the idea soon. Then attach a long piece of cord to the lead—15 or 20 feet—and make him come to you from that distance. When he's coming pretty consistently, have him sit when he reaches you.

Don't be too eager to practice coming on command off lead. Wait till you are certain that you have the dog under perfect control before you try calling him when he's free. Once he gets the idea that he can disobey a command to come and get away with it, your training program will suffer a serious setback. Keep in mind that your dog's life may depend on his immediate response to a command to come when he is called. If he disobeys off lead, put the collar back on and correct him severely with jerks of the lead. He'll get the idea.

It's time for a rest. Brief training periods save both your temper and your pet's. He wants to learn, but training is difficult and tiring, and his concentration span is limited.

In training your dog to come, never use the command when you want to punish him. He should associate the "come" with something pleasant. If he comes very slowly, you can speed his response by pulling on the lead, calling him and running backward with him at a brisk pace.

At first, practice the "sit," "down," "stay" and "come" indoors; then try it in an outdoor area where there are distractions to show the dog that he must obey under any conditions.

HEELING

"Heeling" in dog language means having your pet walk alongside you on your left side, close to your left leg, on lead or off. With patience and effort you can train your dog to walk with you even on a crowded street or in the presence of other dogs. However, don't begin this part of his training too early. Normally, a dog much under 6 months old is just too young to absorb the idea of heeling.

Put the dog at your left side, sitting. Then say "Heel" firmly and start walking at a brisk pace. Do not pull the dog with you, but guide him by tugs on the lead. Keep some slack on the lead and use your left hand to snap the lead for a correction. Always start off with your left foot and after a while the dog

When training your dog to heel, get him to follow your left foot. Keep his attention by continuously talking to him and varying your pace and direction.

will learn to watch that foot and follow it. Keep repeating "Heel" as you walk, snapping the dog back into position if he lags behind or forges ahead. If he gets out of control, reverse your course sharply and snap him along after you. Keep up a running conversation with your dog, telling him what a good fellow he is when he is heeling, letting him know when he is not.

At first limit your heeling practice to about 5 minutes at a time; later extend it to 15 minutes or a half hour. To keep your dog interested, vary the routine. Make right and left turns, change your pace from a normal walk to a fast trot to a very slow walk. Occasionally make a sharp about-face.

Remember to emphasize the word "heel" throughout this practice and to use your voice to let him know that you are displeased when he goes ahead or drops behind or swings wide.

If you are handling him properly, the dog should begin to get the idea of ieeling in about 15 minutes. If you get no response whatever, if the dog runs away from you, fights the lead, gets you and himself tangled in the lead, it may indicate that he is still young, or that you aren't showing him what you expect him to do.

Practicing 15 minutes a day, in 6 or 7 weeks your pet should have developed to the stage where you can remove the lead and he'll heel alongside you. First try throwing the lead over your shoulder or fastening it to your belt, or remove the lead and tie a piece of thin cord (fishing line will do nicely) to his collar. Then try him off lead. Keep his attention by constantly talking; slap your left leg to keep his attention on you. If he breaks away, return to the collar and lead treatment for a while.

"HEEL" MEANS SIT, TOO

To the dog, the command "Heel" will also mean that he has to sit in heel position at your left side when you stop walking—with no additional command from you. As you practice heeling, force him to sit whenever you stop, at first using the word "Sit," then switching over to the command "Heel." He'll soon get the idea and plop his rear end down when you stop and wait for you to give the command "Heel" and start walking again.

TEACHING TO COME TO HEEL

The object of this is for you to stand still, say "Heel!" and have your dog come right over to you and sit by your left knee in heel position. If your dog has been trained to sit without command every time you stop, he's ready for this step.

Sit him in front of and facing you and step back a few feet. Say "Heel" in your most commanding tone of voice and pull the dog into heel position, making him sit. There are several different ways to do this. You can swing the dog around behind you from your right side, behind your back and to heel position. Or you can pull him toward you, keep him on your left side and swing him to heel position. Use your left heel to straighten him out if he begins to sit behind you or crookedly. This may take a little work, but the dog will get the idea if you show him just what you want.

A properly trained dog is a true companion; he can go almost anywhere with you.

When it comes to learning, dogs and children are very similar — patience, understanding and praise for a good job well done bring out the best in them.

THE "STAND"

Your Great Dane should be trained to stand on one spot without moving his feet, and should allow a stranger to run his hands over his body and legs without showing any resentment or fear. Use the same method you used in training him to stay on the sit and down. While walking, place your left hand out, palm toward his nose, and command him to stay. His first impulse will be to sit, so be prepared to stop that by placing your hand under his body. If he's really stubborn, you may have to wrap the lead around his body near his hindquarters and hold him up until he gets the idea that this is different from the command to sit. Praise him for standing and walk to the end of the lead. Correct him strongly if he starts to move. Have a stranger approach him and run his hands over the dog's back and down his legs. Keep him standing until you come back to him. Walk around him from his left side, come to heel position, and let the dog sit as you praise him lavishly.

Great Danes are highly intelligent dogs, and it is up to you to develop your pet's natural aptitudes through training.

RETRIEVING

It's fun to teach your dog to fetch things on command. Use a wooden dumb-bell, a thick dowel stick or a thin, rolled-up magazine. While you have the dog heeling on lead, hold the object in front of him and tease him by waving it in front of his nose. Then say "Take it" and let him grab it. Walk with him while he's carrying it, and then say "Give" and take it from his mouth. If he drops it first, pick it up and tease him until he takes it again and holds it until you remove it.

With the dog still on lead, throw the object a few feet in front of him and encourage him to pick it up and hold it. If he won't give it up when you want it, don't have a tug-of-war. Just blow into his nostrils and he'll release his hold. Then praise him as if he had given it to you willingly.

Don't become discouraged if he seems slow in getting the idea of retrieving. Sometimes it takes several months before the dog will go after an object and bring it to you, but, with patience and persistence on your part, he'll succeed.

Once he gets the habit of retrieving, try throwing the object over a low hurdle and send him over to pick it up and bring it to you. He should jump the hurdle, get it, jump back over and sit in front of you with the object in his mouth.

Don't expect to accomplish all the training overnight. Generally a dog-training school will devote about 10 weeks, with one session a week, to all this training. Between lessons the dogs and their masters are expected to work about 15 minutes every day on the exercises.

It's an exciting feat for your Dane to retrieve an object for you by going over a hurdle. It's excellent exercise as well.

If you'd like more detailed information on training your dog, you'll find it in the pages of HOW TO HOUSEBREAK AND TRAIN YOUR DOG, a Sterling-T.F.H. book.

There are dog-training classes in all parts of the country, some sponsored by the local A.S.P.C.A. A free list of dog-training clubs and schools is available from the Gaines Dog Research Center, 250 Park Avenue, New York, New York.

If you feel that you lack the time or the skill to train your dog yourself, there are professional dog trainers who will do it for you, but basically dog training is a matter of training *you* and your dog to work together as a team, and if you don't do it yourself you will miss a lot of fun.

ADVANCED TRAINING AND OBEDIENCE TRIALS

Once you begin training your Great Dane and see how well he does, you'll probably be bitten by the "obedience bug"—the desire to enter him in obedience trials held under American Kennel Club license. Most dog shows now include obedience classes at which your dog can qualify for his "degrees" to demonstrate his usefulness as a companion dog, not merely as a pet or show dog.

The A.K.C. obedience trials are divided into three classes: Novice, Open and Utility.

In the Novice Class, the dog will be judged on the following basis:

Test	Maximum Score
Heel on leash	35
Stand for examination by judge	30
Heel free—off leash	45
Recall (come on command)	30
1-minute sit (handler in ring)	30
3-minute down (handler in ring)	30
Maximum total score	200

If the dog "qualifies" in three different shows by earning at least 50 per cent of the points for each test, with a total of at least 170 for the trial, he has earned the Companion Dog degree and the letters C.D. are entered in the stud book after his name.

After the dog has qualified as a C.D., he is eligible to enter the Open Class competition where he will be judged on this basis:

Test	Maximum Score
Heel free	40
Drop on recall	30
Retrieve (wooden dumbbell) on flat	25
Retrieve over obstacle (hurdle)	35
Broad jump	20
3-minute sit (handler out of ring)	25
5-minute down (handler out of ring)	25
Maximum total score	200

Again he must qualify in three shows for the C.D.X. (Companion Dog Excellent) title and then is eligible for the Utility Class where he can earn the Utility Dog degree in these rugged tests:

Test	Maximum Score
Scent discrimination (picking up article handled by master from group of articles)—Article 1	20
Scent discrimination—Article 2	20
Scent discrimination—Article 3	20
Seek back (picking up article dropped by handler)	30
Signal exercise (heeling, etc., on hand signal only)	35
Directed jumping (over hurdle and bar jump)	40
Group examination	35
Maximum total score	200

For more complete information about these obedience trials, write to the American Kennel Club, 221 Park Avenue South, New York 3, N.Y., and ask for their free booklet "Regulations and Standards for Obedience Trials." Spayed females and dogs that are disqualified from breed shows because of physical defects are eligible to compete in these trials.

Besides the formal A.K.C. obedience trials, there are informal "match" shows in which dogs compete for ribbons and inexpensive trophies. These shows are run by local Great Dane clubs and by all-breed obedience clubs, and in many localities the A.S.P.C.A. and other groups conduct their own obedience shows. Your local pet shop or kennel can keep you informed about such shows in your vicinity and you will find them listed in the different dog magazines or in the pet column of your local paper.

6. Caring for the Female and Raising Puppies

Whether or not you bought your female dog intending to breed her, some preparation is necessary when and if you decide to take this step.

If you are a member of the Great Dane Club of America, you have promised to maintain quality standards and refrain from crossbreeding.

WHEN TO BREED

It is usually best to breed on the second or third season. Plan in advance the time of year which is best for you, taking into account where the puppies will be born and raised. You will keep them until they are at least 6 weeks old, and a litter of husky pups takes up considerable space by then. Other considerations are selling the puppies (Christmas vs. springtime sales), your own vacation, and time available to care for them. You'll need at least an hour a day to feed and clean up after the mother and puppies but probably it will take you much longer—with time out to admire and play with them!

CHOOSING THE STUD

You can plan to breed your female about 6½ months after the start of her last season, although a variation of a month or two either way is not unusual. Choose the stud dog and make arrangements well in advance. If you are breeding for show stock, which may command better prices, a mate should be chosen with an eye to complementing the deficiencies of your female. If possible, they should have several ancestors in common within the last two or three generations, as such combinations generally "click" best. He should have a good show record or be the sire of show winners if old enough to be proven.

The owner of such a male usually charges a fee for the use of the dog. The fee varies. This does not guarantee a litter, but you generally have the right to breed your female again if she does not have puppies. In some cases the owner of the stud will agree to take a choice puppy in place of a stud fee. You should settle all details beforehand, including the possibility of a single surviving puppy, deciding the age at which he is to make his choice and take the pup, and so on.

If you want to raise a litter "just for the fun of it" and plan merely to make use of an available male Great Dane, the most important point is temperament. Make sure the dog is friendly as well as healthy, because a bad disposition could appear in his puppies, and this is the worst of all traits in a dog destined to be a pet. In such cases a "stud fee puppy," not necessarily the choice of the litter, is the usual payment.

PREPARATION FOR BREEDING

Before you breed your female, make sure she is in good health. She should be neither too thin nor too fat. Any skin disease *must* be cured, before it can be passed on to the puppies. If she has worms she should be wormed before being bred or within three weeks afterward. It is generally considered a good idea to revaccinate her against distemper and hepatitis before the puppies are born. This will increase the immunity the puppies receive during their early, most vulnerable period.

The female will probably be ready to breed 12 days after the first colored discharge. You can usually make arrangements to board her with the owner of the male for a few days, to insure her being there at the proper time, or you can take her to be mated and bring her home the same day. If she still appears receptive she may be bred again two days later. However, some females never show signs of willingness, so it helps to have the experience of a breeder. Usually the second day after the discharge changes color is the proper time, and she may be bred for about three days following. For an additional week or so she may have some discharge and attract other dogs by her odor, but can seldom be bred.

THE FEMALE IN WHELP

You can expect the puppies nine weeks from the day of breeding, although 61 days is as common as 63. During this time the female should receive normal care and exercise. If she was overweight, don't increase her food at first; excess weight at whelping time is bad. If she is on the thin side build her up, giving some milk and biscuit at noon if she likes it. You may add one of the mineral and vitamin supplements to her food to make sure that the puppies will be healthy. As her appetite increases, feed her more. During the last two weeks the puppies grow enormously and she will probably have little room for food and less appetite. She should be tempted with meat, liver and milk, however.

As the female in whelp grows heavier, cut out violent exercise and jumping. Although a dog used to such activities will often play with the children or run around voluntarily, restrain her for her own sake.

PREPARING FOR THE PUPPIES

Prepare a whelping box a few days before the puppies are due, and allow the mother to sleep there overnight or to spend some time in it during the day to become accustomed to it. Then she is less likely to try to have her pups under the front porch or in the middle of your bed. A variety of places will serve, such as a corner of your cellar, garage, or an unused room. If the weather is warm, a large outdoor doghouse will do, well protected from rain or draft. A whelping box serves to separate mother and puppies from visitors and other distractions. The walls should be high enough to restrain the puppies, yet allow the mother to get away from the puppies after she has fed them. Six by eight feet is minimum size, and one-foot walls will keep the pups in until they begin to climb, when it should be built up. Then the puppies really need more room anyway, so double the space with a very low partition down the middle and you will find them naturally housebreaking themselves.

Layers of newspaper spread over the whole area will make excellent bedding and be absorbent enough to keep the surface warm and dry. They should be removed daily and replaced with another thick layer. An old quilt or washable blanket makes better footing for the nursing puppies than slippery newspaper during the first week, and is softer for the mother.

Be prepared for the actual whelping several days in advance. Usually the female will tear up papers, refuse food and generally act restless. These may be false alarms; the real test is her temperature, which will drop to below 100° about 12 hours before whelping. Take it with a rectal thermometer morning and evening, and put her in the pen, looking in on her frequently, when her temperature goes down.

WHELPING

Usually little help is needed but it is wise to stay close to make sure that the mother's lack of experience does not cause an unnecessary accident. Be ready to help when the first puppy arrives, for it could smother if she does not break the membrane enclosing it. She should start right away to lick the puppy, drying and stimulating it, but you can do it with a soft rough towel, instead. The afterbirth should follow the birth of each puppy, attached to the puppy by the long umbilical cord. Watch to make sure that each is expelled, anyway, for retaining this material can cause infection. In her instinct for cleanliness the mother will probably eat the afterbirth after biting the cord. One or two will not hurt her; they stimulate milk supply as well as labor for remaining pups. But too many can make her lose appetite for the food she needs to feed her pups and regain her strength. So remove the rest of them along with the wet newspapers and keep the pen dry and clean to relieve her anxiety.

If the mother does not bite the cord, or does it too close to the body, take over the job, to prevent an umbilical hernia. Tearing is recommended, but you can cut it, about two inches from the body, with a sawing motion of scissors, sterilized in alcohol. Then dip the end in a shallow dish of iodine; the cord will dry up and fall off in a few days.

The puppies should follow each other at intervals of not more than half an hour. If more time goes past and you are sure there are still pups to come, a brisk walk outside may start labor again. If she is actively straining without producing a puppy it may be presented backward, a so-called "breech" or upside-down birth. Careful assistance with a well-soaped finger to feel for the puppy or ease it back may help, but never attempt to pull it by force against the mother. This could cause serious damage, so let an expert handle it.

If anything seems wrong, waste no time in calling your veterinarian, who can examine her and if necessary give hormones which will bring the remaining puppies. You may want his experience in whelping the litter even if all goes well. He will probably prefer to have the puppies born at his hospital rather than to get up in the middle of the night to come to your home. The mother would, no doubt, prefer to stay at home, but you can be sure she will get the best of care in his hospital. If the puppies are born at home and all goes as it should, watch the mother carefully afterward.

For the first few weeks the mother probably won't want to be away from her pups for more than a couple of minutes. Don't handle them too much if your interference seems to make her nervous.

WEANING THE PUPPIES

Hold each puppy to a breast as soon as he is dry, for a good meal without competition. Then he may join his littermates in the basket, out of his mother's way while she is whelping. Keep a supply of evaporated milk on hand for emergencies, or later weaning. A supplementary feeding often helps weak pups over the hump. Keep track of birth weights, and take weekly readings; it will furnish an accurate record of the pups' growth and health.

After the puppies have arrived, take the mother outside for a walk and drink, and then allow her to take care of them. She will probably not want to stay away more than a minute or two for the first few weeks. Be sure to keep water available at all times, and feed her milk or broth frequently, as she needs liquids to produce milk. Encourage her to eat, with her favorite foods, until she asks for it of her own accord. She will soon develop a ravenous appetite and should have at least two large meals a day, with dry food available in addition.

Prepare a warm place to put the puppies after they are born to keep them dry and help them to a good start in life. Cover an electric heating pad or hot-water bottle with flannel and put it in the bottom of a cardboard box. Set the box near the mother so that she can see her puppies. She will usually allow you to help, but don't take the puppies out of sight, and let her handle things if your interference seems to make her nervous.

If the mother is normally healthy after whelping puppies and has ample milk supply for the number of puppies in the litter, it is wise to let them nurse on her until they are three to four weeks of age. If feasible, keep the mother with her puppies until they are five or six weeks of age. As long as they nurse on the mother, puppies are less vulnerable to disease.

For bottle feeding of puppies in the event of illness or death of their mother, it is wise to have an experienced breeder or veterinarian recommend the formula. Whenever possible, it is better to locate a foster mother for the puppies. The foster mother does not necessarily have to be a Great Dane or a large breed of dog.

Be sure that all the puppies are getting enough to eat. If the mother sits or stands, instead of lying still to nurse, the probable cause is scratching from the puppies' nails. You can remedy this by clipping them, as you do hers. Manicure scissors will do for these tiny claws. Some breeders advise disposing of the smaller or weaker pups in a large litter, as the mother has trouble in handling more than six or seven. But you can help her out by preparing an extra puppy box or basket. Leave half the litter with the mother and the other half in a warm place, changing off at two-hour intervals at first. Later you may change them less frequently, leaving them all together except during the day. Try supplementary feeding, too; as soon as their eyes open, at about two weeks, they will lap from a dish, anyway.

While they continue to drink their mother's milk, Great Dane puppies should be given additional nourishment, starting about the twelfth day after birth. Feed each puppy about a level teaspoon of puréed beef—fresh, lean chopped beef put through a mixer until it is creamy smooth like peanut butter—or buy prepared baby meats in jars. Do this two or three times a day.

At three weeks of age, add a tablespoon of condensed milk, diluted with a tablespoon of hot water, and a tablespoon of Pablum. Increase puréed beef to one tablespoon. This should be fed twice each day to each puppy in addition to the mother's milk.

Until they learn to lap it is best to feed one or two at a time, because they are more likely to walk into it than to eat. Hold the saucer at chin level, and let them gather around, keeping paws out of the dish.

Don't leave water with them all the time; at this age they play with everything and they will use it as a wading pool. They can drink all they need if it is offered several times a day, after meals.

As the puppies grow up the mother will go into the pen only to nurse them, first sitting up and then standing. To dry her up completely, keep the mother away for longer periods; after a few days of part-time nursing she can stay away for longer periods, and then completely. The little milk left will be reabsorbed.

AIRING THE PUPPIES

The puppies may be put outside, unless it is too cold, as soon as their eyes are open, and will benefit from the sunlight and vitamins. A rubber mat or newspapers underneath will protect them from cold or damp.

You can expect the pups to need at least one worming before they are ready to go to new homes, so take a stool sample to your veterinarian before they are three weeks old. If one puppy has worms all should be wormed. Follow the veterinarian's advice, and this applies also to vaccination. If you plan to keep a pup you will want to vaccinate him at the earliest age possible, so his littermates should be done at the same time.

7. Showing Your Great Dane

You probably think that your Great Dane is the best in the country and possibly in the world, but before you enter the highly competitive world of the show, get some unbiased expert opinions. Compare your dog against standards on pages 9-15. If a Great Dane club in your vicinity is holding a match show, enter your dog and see what the judges think of him. If he places in a few match shows, then you might begin seriously considering the big-time shows. Visit a few as a spectator first and make careful mental notes of what is required of the handlers and the dogs. Watch how the experienced handlers manage their dogs to bring out their best points. See how they use pieces of liver to "bait" the dogs and keep them alert in the ring. If experts think your dog has the qualities to make a champion, you might want to hire a professional handler to show him.

ADVANCE PREPARATION

Before you go to a show your dog should be trained to gait at a trot beside you, with head up and in a straight line. In the ring you will have to gait around the edge with other dogs and then individually up and down the center runner. In addition the dog must stand for examination by the judge, who will look at him closely and feel his head and body structure. He should be taught to stand squarely, hind feet slightly back, head up on the alert. He must hold the pose when you place his feet and show animation for a piece of boiled liver in your hand or a toy mouse thrown in front of you.

Showing requires practice training sessions in advance. Get a friend to act as judge and set the dog up and "show" him for a few minutes every day.

Fortunately, the Great Dane requires little special grooming for his show appearance. Brush him, see that his nails are trimmed, and use the hand-rub mentioned earlier to bring out the sheen in his coat.

The day before the show, pack your kit. You will want to take a water dish and bottle of water for your dog (so that he won't be affected by a change in drinking water, and you won't have to go look for it). A chain or leash to fasten him to the bench, or stall, where he must remain during the show, and a show lead should be included, as well as grooming tools. The show lead is a thin nylon or cord collar and leash combined, which doesn't detract from the dog's appearance as much as a clumsier chain and lead. Also put in the identification ticket sent by the show superintendent, noting the time you must be there and the place where the show will be held, as well as the time of judging.

THE DAY OF THE SHOW

Don't feed your dog the morning of the show, or give him at most a light

(Above) The author trots down the ring with Ch. Honey Hollow Stormi Rudio at the '59 Westminster show. Stormi was the first Great Dane ever to win Working Group and he was runner-up for Best in Show.

(Below) Stormi being awarded one of his many Best-in-Shows in all-breed competition. Miss Basquette has won many laurels herself—some readers may remember her as a popular star in silent movies.

meal. He will be more comfortable in the car on the way, and will show more enthusiastically. When you arrive at the show grounds an official veterinarian will check your dog for health, and then you should find his bench and settle him there. Locate the ring where Great Danes will be judged, take the dog to the exercise ring to relieve himself, and give him a small drink of water. After a final grooming, you have only to wait until your class is called. It is your responsibility to be at the ring at the proper time.

Then, as you step into the ring, try to keep your knees from rattling too loudly. Before you realize it you'll be out again, perhaps back with the winners for more judging and finally —with luck—it will be all over and you'll have a ribbon and an armful of silver trophies. And a very wonderful dog!

You will be handsomely rewarded when your Great Dane stands proudly in front of the ribbons and trophies you knew all along he would win.